The History of Brazil

A Fascinating Guide to Brazilian History

By
David Robbins

professional before attempting any techniques outlined in this book.

By reading this document, the reader agrees that under no circumstances is the author responsible for any losses, direct or indirect, that are incurred as a result of the use of the information contained within this document, including, but not limited to, errors, omissions, or inaccuracies.

Table of Contents

PRECOLONIAL BRAZIL

Brazil is the largest country in South America. In fact it is so large that it takes up half the continent's land mass. Its sheer size is also impressive on the world scale. Only four other countries, the United States, China, Russia and Canada, are bigger. Its presence on the continent is so substantial that it borders every country except Chile and Ecuador.

But it's not just Brazil's scale that impresses; it is one of the most ecologically diverse nations on the planet. Environments in the country range from rainforest to wetlands, mountains to savannas. It also has an unbelievably vibrant culture fueled by a complicated history and an equally diverse populace.

Where did it all start for Brazil? It started like most countries in the New World. Tribes of indigenous peoples inhabited Brazil long before the arrival of any European explorers and/or colonizers. And like any other country in the New World, that era was complex.

What is now known as Brazil was inhabited by thousands of tribes. In the Amazon Basin alone there were up to or maybe more than four million people. There's no way to know for sure, especially after the arrival of Europeans and a burgeoning slave trade dwindled those numbers. The rainforest and the Amazon River provided and could sustain a large population of indigenous peoples.

To understand life in Precolonial Brazil, you first have to break down the land to distinct regions, each with different strengths and weaknesses, each with tribes whose ways of life depended on the topography and food available to them. The three main regions were the Atlantic seaboard, which ranged from the Rio Grande do Sul and Bahia. Then there was the Planalto Brasileiro or central plateau (central highlands), and then the Amazon Basin.

Serving as a humungous draining basin for the Amazon River, the Amazon Basin was marked by lowland dense forests. Most tribes, like the Arawak and Carib, depended on farming to survive. They hunted as well, but that could only sustain limited-sized tribes.

The Planalto Brasileiro was perhaps the biggest part of Brazil. It spans the Eastern, Southern and Central portions of the country. Mostly covered in forests and host to highly fertile lands, it had a high concentration of agricultural-based tribes and an unknown amount of plant, animal and insect species. Though the ecological variety waned after the rival of the Portuguese, the lands were still very fertile.

The Atlantic seaboard was about 7,300 hundred kilometers of coastline. Before European explorers and the colonization of Brazil, it was blanketed by the Atlantic Forest and pine forests. Like much of the country, the seaboard was thick with fauna, flora and animal life. Much of that went extinct along with the trees after rapid deforestation reduced the once extensive forests to less than eight percent of its original state.

Tribes in Precolonial Brazil varied greatly, as did their ways of life. Some were hunter-gatherers, others scavengers or harvesters. The rarer tribes practiced cannibalism. It is hard to know for sure the extent of the larger tribes' reach and in-depth histories due to the lack of archaeological evidence. Most of our modern information came from the first Europeans to land in Brazil: the Portuguese. They described two main tribes, the Tupi and the Guarani.

The Tupi originated in the nearby Paraguay Basin. From there they migrated and invaded the Brazilian Atlantic Ocean coastline. There are conflicting theories as to why they did so, but the answers might've been found in their known way of life. They were practicing cannibals.

7

In order to carry out their religious and ritualistic beliefs, the Tupi needed prisoners. So they moved north. They arrived in Brazil in small groups and made their way out to the Atlantic coastline.

There were seventy-six known tribes that spoke the Tupi language. Every tribe lived communal-style in large long houses. Each long house housed up to thirty families. Living so close together, sleeping next to each other, the Tupi quickly formed and maintained strong bonds within their tribes -- ones they fiercely protected.

Despite their wooden long houses, the Tupi were far from sedentary. They were semi-nomadic, moving every five years or less, sticking close to the coast. Though cannibalistic, they thankfully did not depend on people for food, at least not to eat them. Those practices were more for ritual than subsistence. They hunted, fished, scavenged and gathered.

With their rituals and way of life came violence. The Tupi were aggressive. Expansion was always one of their prime directives as a people. A lack of a proper structure of hierarchy meant that inter-tribal warfare was very common. Though by no means "savages" the Tupi understandably gave the ignorant Portuguese that impression.

The Guarani, a name given to them by Europeans --
Jesuit missionaries to be exact -- were similar but at the
same time very different than the Tupi. Like them they
lived in communal long houses. Like them they were
cannibals, although evidence points to them being a little
more selective on whom and when they ate human beings.

Unlike the Tupi, the Guarani were not nomadic.
They focused on agriculture, growing food such as maize
and honey. Unfortunately, they also lacked a written
language and history. Most of Guarani tradition and
culture was passed on orally, making recovery of it today
near impossible from anyone other than European
accounts.

Prior to the arrival of the first European explorers
and the colonization of Brazil by the Portuguese, the
country was home to a diverse array of tribes with an even
more diverse array of cultures. Those cultures, not carried
on by any written language, became lost to the disease,
war and slavery brought on wooden ships across the
Atlantic from Europe. Even today a relatively small
amount of information has survived about the indigenous
peoples of Brazil.

COLONIAL BRAZIL

It isn't exactly clear which European explorer was first to set foot in what is now modern day Brazil. Historians cannot agree on which one of three different men and their parties staked claim to that "accomplishment." Most believe it was Pedro Alvarez Cabral, the man credited by Portugal. Others say it was Duarte Pacheco Pereira. Another camp believed that the first explorer was Vicente Yanez Pinzon.

Vicente Yanez Pinzon, born in Palos de la Frontera, Spain, came from nobility. The conquistador actually captained the "Nina" that took part in Christopher Columbus's first voyage to the New World. Unlike his brother, Martin, he stayed loyal and with Columbus's fleet until the completion of their journey.

Though he did not desert the mission during Christopher Columbus's voyage, Vicente Yanez Pinzon had a major point of contention with the credited discoverer of the New World. He believed, despite his brother Martin Pinzon leaving to try and find gold and riches in Caribbean, he deserved equal credit for the monumental discovery. Perhaps fueled by his family's perceived mistreatment, he was determined to set out, explore and make discoveries of his own.

With a newly restored and outfitted ship, his brother's "The Pinta," Vicente Yanez Pinzon set off on his own voyage in 1499. Eventually he landed in what is now modern day Pernanbuco, Brazil. He named it Cabo Santa Maria de la Consolacian. He and his crew continued north until they reached the Amazon River.

Having gone about fifty miles up the river, Vicente Yanez Pinzon was and is credited as the first European to explore the Amazon River. Though it was far from his only discovery, it was his most famous. Gone from the brother of a disgraced explorer to making an important find for Portugal, he came home years later a distinguished hero.

Some historians believe that it was Portuguese Duarte Pacheco Pereira who was the first European explorer to discover Brazil. The so-called "Achilles of Portugal" came from prestigious roots. He was a squire in the King of Portugal's court. He explored the extensive Western coast of Africa and traversed Cape of Good Hope. Eventually he was named the official geographer for the crown.

By some disputed accounts, Duarte Pacheco Pereira beat Amerigo Vespucci in the discovery of Brazil. It is said that he may have discovered the coasts of Marajo Island,

Para, Maranhao and the mouth of the mighty Amazon River back in 1498, almost a full year before Vespucci in 1499 and Vincente Yanez Pinzon in 1450, though not all historians agree that this is the case.

Duarte Pacheco Pereira's alleged discovery of Brazil was questioned heavily in the book "Foundations of the Portuguese Empire." The best and most-quoted excerpt from the book written by contemporary British and Portuguese historians reads:

"What really is important," Duarte Leite says, "is to know whether Pacheco arrived in Brazil before Alvares Cabral (April 22, 1500). In agreement with Luciano Pereira, such modern Portuguese historians as Faustino da Fonseca, Brito Rebelo, Lopes de Mendonça, and Jaime Cortesão say he did. . . as does Vignaud; and I believe he does not lack supporters in Brazil." "However," says Leite, "if Pacheco did discover areas east of the Line of Demarcation and did bring back news of this to [King] Manuel [of Portugal], the reason which induced Don Manuel to keep secret. . . such an important discovery escapes me. As soon as Cabral returned in 1501, Manuel announced the discovery of Brazil to Ferdinand and Isabella of Spain. Why would he not in 1499, after the return of Vasco da Gama, make a similar announcement if Pacheco had already discovered Brazil? No objection could come on the part of Spain, given the division made by the Treaty of Tordesillas, as indeed none came in 1501 when Cabral's discovery was announced. I am persuaded that Pacheco neither discovered Brazil in 1498 nor was present two years later at its discovery by Cabral."

After his famous exploration of India and the Battle of Cochin, Duarte Pachecho Pereira was commissioned to pursue privateers and pirates, assigned a governorship and wrote several books. With success came more than his fair share of enemies. Accusations of corruption and treason even had him locked up in Portugal for several years.

Born in 1467 or 1468 (historians aren't sure which year) in Belmonte, Portugal, Pedro Alvares Cabral was one of the most famous and accomplished Portuguese explorers of all time. Though he wasn't the first European or even Portuguese explorer to step foot in what is now Brazil, he was the one to go further inland and officially claim it for the crown. So how did that come about?

With a fleet of thirteen ships and 1,200 men, Pedro Alvares Cabral set off from the Portuguese capital of Lisbon on March 9, 1500. The plan wasn't to go find new islands or countries of the crown but instead to follow Vasco de Gama's route south, around Africa to India to engage in trade. But his expedition went too far south after passing the Canary Islands. That brought him to lands unknown to most Europeans in South America.

When he realized that he did not land in India but instead in new undiscovered lands, Pedro Alvares Cabral took full advantage of his own mistake. His fleet made anchor in Port Segundo. Once there he insisted on going a little inland into the beach and erected a cross proclaiming the land as property of Portugal and the church.

Pedro Alvares Cabral didn't immediately leave, however. He stuck around for a little bit, ten days to be exact. After sending a ship back to Portugal to inform them of his new discovery, he spent the rest of his time there in Terra de Vera Cruz. During his time there he had numerous interactions with the native population. He wanted to not only keep the peace with them but also introduce those he saw as "savages" to Catholicism. The indigenous people, not recognizing the threat that his arrival posed, were very receptive and curious about these strange people and their strange religious beliefs.

The journey did not end in Brazil for Pedro Alvares Cabral and his crew. Straight from Terra de Vera Cruz, he and his fleet set off back to their original mission, to reach

India and establish trade routes for the Portuguese crown. But things went far from planned as the journey almost ended during the trip to the Cape of Good Hope in Africa.

Pedro Alvares Cabral and his fleet got caught in a series of terrible storms near the African coast. Four of his ships sank in the tumultuous weather, their entire crews drowning beneath the churning waves. Despite this great loss, the fleet continued on its mission. Unfortunately for Pedro Alvares Cabral and his crew, that's not where the bad fortune ended.

Finally in September 1500, Alvares reached Calicut, India. He engaged in disputes with Arab traders in India and at one point had several of his men killed. In retaliation, Pedro Alvares Cabral invaded a local city, captured ten Arab ships and murdered their entire crews. He returned a year later to Lisbon, Portugal, and was met with a mixed reception. Yes, he discovered Brazil, a soon-to-be-prosperous land for the crown, but his subsequent time in India worsened relations with Arab traders who were essential for successful trade routes in Asia.

After the discovery of Brazil, the bountiful country was open for colonization. Portugal, in competition with the Spanish and British for new territories, made the Amazon dominated lands a priority. Soon a wave of colonists would land in this New World ready to settle it no matter the cost.

You discuss the colonization of Brazil without first acknowledging and going over the Treaty of Tordesillas. After the discoveries of late fifteenth century explorers like Christopher Columbus, Spain and Portugal came together to reach an agreement about how to partition and deal with new lands outside of Europe. Signed in on June 7, 1494, the treaty kept a sense of order during a wild time of rapid discovery by the two Empires. But the treaty excluded other world powers such as the British who had no qualms about making incursions into either side's territories.

Unlike some empires at the time, the Portuguese did not engage in colonialism for new lands for people to settle in, but primarily just to find new resources and make money. Being such a small country their population was low and they couldn't hope to maintain fully populated colonies in the New World. For the Portuguese, Brazil and the Amazon River represented money.

The strategy of the Portuguese at the time of the discovery of Brazil was fairly simple. First, they'd scout out a good location to establish a trade fort. Then they'd conquer the area and set up said trade fort. Usually along rivers or coastlines, these forts would then facilitate a steady stream of goods out of the trade fort to surrounding colonies and then back to Portugal.

Portugal's initial interest in Brazil was brazil wood. This led to conflict with the French who did not adhere to the Treaty of Tordesillas and did all they could to extract as much of the valuable resource as possible. After some fighting and skirmishes over the brazil wood, the Portuguese decided to send a much larger force of colonists and soldiers to kick out the French and form a more solid footing in the country. In 1530, an expedition led by Martim Afonso de Sousa managed to permanently expel the French, patrol the coast, and establish several towns and trading posts along it.

Eventually the export of brazil wood was replaced with the more profitable crop of sugarcane. Without the needed number of colonists, the empire turned to slavery to work the plantation and farms in Brazil. That led to the first breaking of the borders established by the Treaty of Tordesillas. Slave hunters expanded their search area to populate and work these new vast sugarcane plantations.

At first, Brazil was colonized by a system of captaincies. These were medieval-style feudal mini-governments meant to save money in the New World by handing over the rule and the responsibility of funding these captaincies by private businessmen and nobility. There were fifteen in Brazil, each specialized in a valuable resource for Portugal.

The system of captaincies for the most part failed, however. There were many reasons why they failed. Chief among them were shipwrecks, resistance from indigenous tribes, and disputes among the colonists and captaincies themselves. Two out of the original fifteen survived.

Pernambuco, the most successful captaincy, founded by Vicente Yanez Pinzon, headed by Duarte Coehlo prospered in trading sugar. Highly valued in Europe it was Brazil's number one export for over one hundred and fifty years. The other surviving captaincy, Sao Vicente, owned by Martim Afonso Sousa also produced sugar. But Sao Vicente's main product was human beings, slaves consisting of the indigenous population.

With the captaincies failing and the reintroduction of France as a threat, King John III decided to send a large fleet in 1549 led by Tome de Sousa to reestablish the crown's royal rule of their Brazilian colony. His mission was to create a central government and regain order in the sugar cash cow to the southwest.

The first Governor-General of Brazil, Tome de Sousa founded the colony's capital city of Salvador de Bahia in the Northeast, what is now Bahia. Tome de Sousa set about visiting, repairing and reorganizing the various captaincies to restore their economic and trade output as well as establish a connected network that was more efficient and under his and Salvador de Bahia's rule. Along with the capital being established, the church made its mark in 1551 when it founded the Diocese of Sao Salvador de Bahia.

The importance of Tome de Sousa's reign and official introduction of Western religion, Catholicism, to Brazil cannot be overlooked. With him came the first groups of Jesuits to the country. Their spreading of the Catholic faith in the young country became a central factor in the colony going forward.

Jesuits were unique among colonists as they sought to connect and better understand the native population instead of fighting them. They learned from these indigenous tribes, their language, customs and religions while also teaching their own ways in return. There was an observable sharp decline in conflicts between these tribes and the Portuguese after the arrival of the Jesuits.

Not only did the Jesuits foster a deeper understanding and cooperation between the indigenous people of Brazil and the Portuguese, they fought against what they saw as injustices. Primarily, they fought against slavery and slavers. That brought them into conflict with other colonists who insisted that slave labor was essential to their plantations. But Jesuits, confident in their beliefs or cooperation with the natives, insisted on trying to end their state of enslavement.

The Jesuits, however, were not all good nor a blessing to the indigenous people of Brazil. They inadvertently spread disease among the natives, leading to mass infections and deaths. They interfered in some ancient ways of life and cultures. Plus, they were only against the enslavement of those from the Americas. No action was taken to try and end the enslavement and import of African slaves.

Following Governor-General Tome de Sousa was a man by the name of Duarte de Costa. His often violent rule was from 1553-1557. It was marked by various conflicts with indigenous tribes, angry about the invaders and the enslavement of their people by the Portuguese.

The conflicts under de Costa's rule weren't limited to the natives, however. He clashed with colonists and even the church itself. This clash with the church came after he took the blame for a Catholic bishop who was attacked and eaten by Caete natives after a 1556 shipwreck.

After Duarte de Costa's arduous rule as Governor-General of Brazil, a third man, Mem de Sa, was appointed the position. During his nearly two decade rule, Mem de Sa managed to defeat and squash the indigenous opposition in the country and expel troublemaking French colonists. His nephew, Estacio de Sa, founded Rio de Janeiro in 1565.

Eventually the sheer size of Brazil, which was still growing, necessitated that it be split in half with two capitals and two governors. So in 1621, King Phillip II founded the states of Brazil, with a capital of Salvador, and Maranhao, with a capital of Sao Luis.

Bereft of gold and silver, sugar was the main cash crop of Brazil and the prime reason for Portuguese and other European countries' interest in the vast, wild country. Starting in the mid-sixteenth century, sugarcane plantations and mills soon spread and dominated the fertile soils. From about 1530-1700, Brazil was in the so-called "Sugar Age."

At first, the Portuguese depended on slaves from the indigenous population to work their sugar plantations. But opposition from these tribes and from the newly introduced Jesuits made them not abandon slavery but turn to the African slave trade to work their lands. Repercussions of this practice can be seen today in modern Brazil, which has a heavy African diaspora.

Portugal, a world power at the time, had multiple commercial enterprises in Western Africa that provided a steady stream of slaves. After their nightmarish journeys on dirty, dark, crowded ships to Brazil, these slaves were expected to do most if not all of the work for the colonists and regularly harvest sugarcane to be processed in or out of country and sent back to Europe to be sold. Though these human rights violations were egregious, they were far from the only European power in central and South America to do so. Britain, Spain, Netherlands and France all followed a similar blueprint to work farms across those regions.

The Sugar Age was essential in building up a very young Brazil. Though it was far from the only European colony to produce sugar and sugarcane, the Portuguese dominated the market. Along with the influx of money and slaves, it gave their empire more power and influence on the world stage. Part of their dominance was   the high quality of the product produced there.

Unfortunately for Brazil and Portugal, their domination of the sugar market wasn't meant to last. French and Dutch colonies in Antilles during the seventeenth and eighteenth centuries not only undercut the Brazilian-produced product, but they were much closer to Europe. Eventually the two rival empires usurped the Portuguese spot atop the sugar throne. Prices in Europe fell, as did the value of Brazil's main cash crop and export.

THE IBERIAN UNION

In 1580, crisis struck in Spain and Portugal. After the demise of Portugal's King Sebastian I in battle in 1578 the crown went to his heir and grand uncle Henry I. When Henry I died in 1580 there was no heir to take the throne. Predictably, this led to extensive in fighting and struggles to claim and legitimatize claims to the crown. Ultimately, a new ruler came from their bigger and more stable neighbor, Spain.

Phillip II of Spain took control over Portugal uniting the two great empires under the flag of the Iberian Union. During the sixty year union the power of the Portuguese empire greatly declined, as did their hold on their colonies worldwide, though this period was profitable for some in the empire.

New Christians greatly benefited from the rule of the Iberian Union. They consisted of converted Jews whose main role in Brazil and the rest of the waning Portuguese Empire was as successful merchants. Their role in this new country, along with Brazil avoiding the Inquisition in Spain and Portugal that decimated many not seen as pure practicing Christians, allowed them to rise to a prominent role in Brazilian society.

On a darker note, the Iberian Union presented new opportunities for other Portuguese merchants in Brazil. Slave traders benefited greatly from the union of two of the biggest players in the slave trade, Portugal and Brazil. The numbers of indigenous and African-born slaves increased several times over, leading to problems with mistreated escaped slaves further down the line.

Reliance on slave labor and their subsequent mistreatment in Brazil led to eventual slave revolts and escapes. Surrounded by dense rainforests, it was relatively easy, compared to most European colonies, for African slaves in Brazil to escape into the wild and never be found by their enslavers.

These runaway slaves often grouped together to create small settlements called quilombos and mocambos. The largest quilombo was called "Quilombo dos Palmares." It is believed that upwards of thousands of escaped slaves and indigenous people lived there during its height during the Dutch incursion into Brazil.

The thriving Quilombo dos Palmares was led first by Ganga Zumba then Ganga Zumbi. They were responsible for both the spiritual and physical defense of the diverse community. Naturally its existence threatened and angered both the Dutch and the Portuguese. Several attempts were made to crush the escaped slave sanctuary. It wasn't until 1695 when a small army led by Domingos Jorge Velho moved on and crushed the settlement, killing Zumbi.

Though the largest quilombo, Quilombo dos Palmares, was destroyed, the impact of their existence is still felt today. Their leaders became folk heroes. Films were made about them and some of them still exist today as small rural farming communities.

One of the most important developments during the time of the Iberian Union was that the Netherlands gained its independence from Spain in 1581. That led to King Phillip II banning any Spanish, Portuguese or colonist traders from dealing with the Dutch. Problem was that the Dutch had already invested significant money and resources in Brazil prior to their independence and had no intention on throwing that all away. Sailors from the island nations were also one of the primary shippers of sugar back to Europe.

Conflict arose between Dutch privateers during the Iberian Union and Brazilian colonists and the Spanish/Portuguese Navy. These privateers led raids along the Brazilian coastline, which eventually led them to Salvador. The Dutch privateer raid on Salvador resulted in the theft and seizure of the gold and silver stores in the city. Eventually the Spanish/Portuguese Navy retook the city but never recovered those valuables.

The Iberian Union was never going to last. This was especially true once King Phillip II died. His successor Philip III raised taxes on Portuguese merchants and he started stripping the country's nobility of their powers. Add to that the lack of Spanish aid to fight the Dutch, who increasingly moved in on Brazil, and the Portuguese inched closer to revolt.

The end for the Iberian Union started with the Catalan Revolt. Taking advantage of the Spaniard preoccupation with the Thirty Year War, conspirators killed the appointed secretary of state and more importantly kidnapped Phillip III's cousin the Duchess of Mantua, who was the acting leader of Portugal. On December 2, 1640 John the 8th Duke of Braganza was proclaimed the new king of Portugal. That sparked a tidal wave of popular support for Portuguese independence from Spain.

A Portuguese Restoration war broke out between Portugal and Spain. Made weaker by having to stretch their military thin in the Thirty Year War, Phillip III's forces struggled to find a decisive victory over their rebellious neighbor. The turning point came when France, England and Germany all sent soldiers to support Portugal, which overwhelmed the Spanish.

The Spanish Empire reached near ruin as its expensive highly unsuccessful campaign against Portugal drained their treasury and planted seeds of descent among the populace. Stubborn, Spain kept fighting two years past the point that defeat was obvious and on the horizon. Eventually Spain gave in and Portugal was given its independence once again. On February 13, 1668, Portugal was officially recognized as its own sovereign independent nation.

NEW HOLLAND/DUTCH BRAZIL

During the turmoil in the Iberian Union, the Netherlands sought to take advantage of the lack of supervision over Brazil. It all began, as it often did, in Europe, after the Dutch gained their Independence from Spain in 1581. Iberian King Phillip II made allowances for the Dutch to sail once a year with a limited fleet to Brazil and back for trade purposes.

At first, the relations between the Iberian Union and the Netherlands in regards to Brazil were civil. Other than the problem of Dutch privateers who did all they could to skirt around the trade restrictions, they formed a treaty to allow more Dutch investment and travel to Brazil as a way to bolster the young country with foreign investment. Chief among them was the Twelve Year Treaty. But as soon as that treaty expired, things for lack of a better term went to hell between the two nations. The Dutch and their Dutch West India Company went about doing all they could to interfere with Spanish and Portuguese trade in Brazil.

In December 1623, the Dutch West India Company set out for Salvador, Brazil, the Brazilian capital, with a plan to take over the city and cement the beginning of their takeover of the Iberian colony. Not only was Salvador immensely important politically for the country but it was also a prime supplier of sugar cane, a valuable crop that the Dutch treasured.

Arriving on May 8, 1624, the West India Company easily took Salvador after its governor immediately surrendered. But they were only able to hold the capital for a little over a year. On April 30, 1625, Iberian Forces of both Spanish and Portuguese troops retook the Brazilian capital.

Things weren't over for either side, though. In 1628, a Spanish fleet was hijacked by the Dutch West India Company in Matanzas Bay. It was a silver convoy hauling a large cargo of the precious metal and provided the needed funds for a second Dutch invasion of Brazil.

Having faced defeat in the Brazilian capital of Salvador, the Dutch decided to shift their sights to another highly lucrative region, Pernambuco. It was, at the time, the largest, most productive and successful sugar producer in the world. That was a target and a prize far too tempting for the angry Dutch to ignore.

In the summer of 1629, a Dutch fleet of sixty five ships was led by West Indian Company's Hendrik Corneliszoon Lonck. First, the West Indian Company captured the city of Olinda on February 16, 1630. It was an essential first step leading to their goal. By March 3, 1630, Hendrik Corneliszoon Lonck's fleet captured Recife, the capital of Pernambuco.

The Portuguese in Brazil didn't simply give up their cities and lands, however. A stiff resistance to the Dutch invasion, led by Matias de Albuquerque, mostly succeeded for a while in stopping the West Indian Company from setting up forts in the country. Eventually though, they were defeated and their enemies went mostly unopposed as they sought to set up settlements out of their newly earned slice of Brazil.

By the time 1634 rolled around, the Dutch controlled coastline from Rio Grande de Norte to Cabo de Santo Agostinho. From there they could keep control of the portion of the ocean they needed to trade and transport sugar. The Dutch weren't done, however. In 1635, they took more valuable Portuguese lands, Arraial do Bom Jesus, Porto Calvo and Fort Nazare.

Though the governments of the Dutch-conquered lands wanted to resist for obvious reasons, the people living there often did not. They actually preferred to live under the foreigners' rule. This was for three reasons. One, they offered religious freedom, far from the strictly Catholic Portuguese beliefs. Two, they guaranteed a semblance of property security, ensuring that it wouldn't just be seized at the whim of a government official. Lastly, these newly conquered Dutch lands were extremely profitable, making them attractive places for merchants to live.

These newly acquired lands in Brazil were named "Nieuw Hollans" or New Holland. The West India Company bequeathed control and governance of these new Dutch colonies to Johan Maurits van Nassau-Siegen. One of Maurit's first moves after gifted power was to capture the Brazilian region of Ceara. Then he immediately sent an expedition across the ocean to capture the West African trading port of Elmina Castle in Ghana. That set up the very profitable Dutch Gold Coast network. He wasn't done, though. Next, he captured the province of Maranhao in order to gain complete control of the coast between the Amazon and Sao Francisco Rivers.

Life under Johan Maurits van Nassau-Siegen was good. A large part of that came from his professed love for Brazil. Through his patronage of famous Dutch painters like Frans Post he had beautiful paintings made of the Brazilian landscapes, diverse population and wildlife. He welcomed naturalists, scientists and biologists to come and study the vast wild rainforests. In fact, his efforts led to the first European publication of scientific information on nature in the Americas, "Historia Naturalis Brasiliae." It continued to be studied for over a century back in their home continent.

Johan Maurits van Nassau-Siegen believed in integrating Brazilians into his new form of local representative government. He also provided protections for different religions, especially Brazilian Jews who were ostracized under Portuguese and Iberian Union rule. In a radical move, he even saw to the facilitation of new Christians being able to revert back to their original Jewish beliefs. Dutch Brazil became a haven for the religious in a time when a person's religion could spark wars (Thirty Year War).

Things changed in Dutch Brazil after the fall of the Iberian Union back in Europe. In 1641, the Portuguese and the Dutch came to truce to temporarily cease all hostilities between the two nations in the colonial nation. And though Johan Maurits van Nassau-Siegen was very successful, the West India Company summoned him back to the Netherlands, forcing him to leave all the good work he did behind.

It was no surprise after the stable presence of Johan Maurits van Nassau-Siegen gone, that Dutch Brazil was thrown into turmoil. It started in June 1645. Some Portuguese farmers in and around Pernambuco, never accepted the new Dutch rule in what they saw as their country. They began to form together to create a small army.

The small army of disgruntled Portuguese farmers attacked and managed to take back the Pernambuco, but not the capital of Recife, which held strong. Their taking back of the region inspired other Portuguese forces in the country to fight back. Later that year, Dutch colonies and forts started falling one by one. They suffered multiple defeats in Fort Maurits, Fort of Porto Calvo, Pontal de Nazare, Sirinhaem and Varzea.

Come 1646, all that the West India Company had left in Brazil were four strongholds along the coast. Chief among them was Recife, which was now almost surrounded by enemies. They sent a reasonable force to reinforce the important city, which helped them withstand Portuguese attacks. But the writing was on the wall. This was especially true because of the

Netherlands's parallel conflict back in Europe with Spain in the Eighty Years War.

After a couple of devastating defeats against the Brazilian Portuguese, the Dutch were against the ropes. Things got really bad after they were defeated for the second time in Guararapes. That devastating loss broke the will of the Dutch army in the New World and opened them up for the upcoming death blow of losing Recife.

Dutch Captain Walter Van Loo was tasked with making a last stand in Recife along with the surviving soldiers from their earlier defeats. Though by all accounts they fought valiantly and fiercely, they lost against a superior enemy. On January 28, 1654, the Portuguese retook Recife and ended Dutch control over any part of Brazil. New Holland was no more.

The ramifications of the fall of New Holland cannot be understated. First, there was the human cost. Having more freedoms under Dutch rule, many native Brazilians and escaped slaves fought for them during their war with Portugal. After losing, they had to face revenge, killing, assaults and seizure of lands. Those Portuguese who had to flee after those areas in Northeast Brazil were taken by the West India Company came back angry and did everything they could to take back what was once theirs, either by force or through litigation.

More than anything else, the fall of New Holland gravely affected the Brazilian economy. This was for a variety of reasons. First, during the fighting, both sides practiced a scorched earth policy. That meant they had to completely rebuild the sugar plantations that were so profitable in the region. Money had to be diverted from investing in the colony to the fight itself. Pernambuco, the most profitable sugar producer in the world never recovered.

As fighting raged in Dutch Brazil, the other colonial powers, Britain and France, made inroads into the sugar industry. The Dutch themselves used their colonies in the Caribbean to start providing the sugar and profits that they lost in Brazil. Before the fall of New Holland, the country produced about eighty percent of the world's sugar. By the end of the war they only produced ten percent. Brazil didn't recover from this until the discovery of gold in the eighteenth century.

GOLD

Traveling inland into Brazil's interior was extremely difficult. Mostly it was due to the terrain and the dangerous insects and wildlife. Portuguese and European explorers in general had a very hard time making significant progress into the Amazon rainforest. Still, brave souls kept trying, hoping to find deposits of precious metals like gold or silver and were met with failure. So colonists focused on building up the coasts and the rich farmlands to facilitate trade of sugar and other goods.

There were two types of expeditions that braved the Amazon rainforest. Entradas were funded by Portugal and had the sole goal of finding precious metals. Bandierantes were privately funded expeditions that also wanted to find precious metals but also looked for and tried to capture native slaves. It was the bandierantes that, in the late seventeenth century, found gold in central Brazil, Minas Gerais.

The discovery of gold in Minas Gerais lit the fuse of a gold rush that would be immeasurably important in the growth and history of Brazil. People were able to move inland and settle the largest, central part of the country. The influx of money in the economy saved it from the turmoil of the end of New Holland and led to industrialization and the first vestiges of modern Brazil.

Back across the Atlantic Ocean in Portugal, news that gold was found in their colony of Brazil was the best possible thing they ever could have heard. Much like the colony, their economy was on the verge of ruins. War with Spain and the Netherlands had drained their treasury and forced them to resort to borrowing money and making cuts. So once they were informed of the find, they went about fully supporting the resulting gold rush.

Almost a half a million Portuguese and another half a million slaves flooded the interior of Brazil and Minas Gerais. Often they abandoned their once-profitable sugar plantations to get their piece of the riches in the country's interior. Institutions and markets, once dependant on agricultural goods, fell to ruin and settlements rapidly started popping up in the areas around the gold mines. Over half of the Brazilian population lived in Southeastern Brazil, where gold was found, by 1725.

The distribution of people in Brazil changed so drastically that it became the most densely populated region in South America at the time. To put it in perspective, the bustling growing New York City in the

United States had less than half the population of Sao Paulo.

With this sudden influx of people, Brazil needed to figure out a way to feed and clothe all these gold miners. Advancements were made in food production and water sanitation during this gold rush period. Infrastructure such as roads, housing and sewage saw drastic improvements and investments to support this new region of the country. And along with the new found money other aspects of the culture like music and the arts benefited.

Once they found precious metals in one part of the country, Brazil and the Portuguese crown wanted to expand their search and stretch the country's boundaries and borders, ignoring the Treaty of Torsedillas. That meant going south. Their only real obstacle in this endeavor was Spain and its far southern colony, Argentina. Specifically, Portugal was interested in the silver mines of Potosi, which is in modern day Bolivia.

Portugal ordered colonial governor Manuel Lobo to occupy a section of the River Plate and set up a settlement there. This was ordered knowing full well that the land they were looking to start a colony in belonged to Spain. Manuel Lobo did exactly that and founded Colonia de

Sacramento in 1679 on the opposite side of the margin from Buenos Aires.

Colonia de Sacramento was an almost fort-like settlement with only three real purposes. Primarily, it was a key stop in the illegal trade of good between the two young countries. Second, it gave them the first foothold into what would become Southern Brazil. Third, it provoked the Spanish, whom they still harbored ill will to.

Naturally, Colonia de Sacramento was not met with open arms by Spain or Argentina. There were several armed conflicts over the fortified settlement. But as those disputes broke out, Portugal went about establishing several more settlements in Southern Brazil, further cementing their claim to their land.

The fighting and skirmishes over the border colonies in Southern Brazil continued until 1750. In 1750, Spain and Portugal signed the Treaty of Madrid. Among the terms they agreed on, both sides would cease hostilities, Portugal was granted huge swaths of land to create Southern Brazil and Spain got what it wanted, ownership over Colonia de Sacramento.

Minas Gerais was not only important for its gold. It was also the stage for a famous conspiracy against colonial authority. Towards the end of the eighteenth century, as the gold mines started to dry up, the possibility of change was in the air.

INDEPENDENCE

Inspired by the Age of Enlightenment and the successful American Revolution in the United States, disgruntled colonialists started to conspire against their Portuguese rulers. Most of them were European educated, affluent, white land owners and politicians in Minas Gerais.

The conspirators were angry with the Portuguese Crown for a variety of reasons. In the wake of declining production from Minas Gerais's gold mines, Portugal had planned on imposing a new policy of forced debt repayment with the threat of serious consequences if those obligations weren't paid. Not only was that seen as not fair but for many, not possible. They also desired the creation of a new republic, free from the chains of the crown and based on Democratic elections. Though it should be mentioned they wanted to keep the slaves.

The rebellion failed before it even began. The Portuguese Colonial government got wind of the conspirators' plans and squashed it in 1789. They rounded them up, including the leader, Joaquim Jose da Silva Xavier (aka Tiradentes). Tiradentes was hanged, drawn and quartered, and shipped around Brazil to display as a warning to any others who desired independence. His co-conspirators were either hanged or sent into exile in Angola, a Portuguese colony in Africa.

Though the Minas Gerais conspiracy failed in twenty to thirty years, Portugal's hold and ownership of Brazil would be released. It started with where many of the colony's troubles started, war in Europe.

In 1807, French conqueror Napoleon Bonaparte wanted to strike a blow to their enemy, England. But instead of attacking them directly, he went after one of their allies, Portugal. At the time, the Portuguese Empire was Prince Regent Joao. He ruled on behalf of his mother, Queen Maria I. Prince Regent Joao had himself and the royal court ferried away to Brazil before the French war machine reached them.

In March 1808, Prince Regent Joao reached the Brazilian capital of Rio de Janeiro. In 1815, he created the United Kingdom of Portugal, Brazil and the Algarves. By doing so he raised Brazil's status, not only in the empire but in the world in general. It was now not just a colony, it was a state on the same level as Portugal itself.

When Queen Maria I died in 1816, Prince Joao stepped up as the undisputed monarch of the Portuguese Empire. He was officially crowned as King Joao VI in 1818 in Rio de Janeiro. This new king wanted to improve his new home leading to some sweeping changes in Brazil.

King Joao VI was on a mission to improve the commerce and industry in Brazil. Some of the measures he took were the creation of medical schools, founding of military academies, improvement of infrastructure, founding of the First Bank of Brazil, and granting the crown's permission to print newspapers and books.

Since it was the city in which he lived and the capital of Brazil, King Joao VI ordered work done there as well. He established the Escola Nacional de Belas Artes, a large and prestigious art academy. The Rio de Janeiro Botanical Gardens were built. In an effort to bring more culture to the young country he also had an opera house built, Teatro Sao Joao.

King Joao VI's many improvements and projects during his reign in Brazil helped the country stand on its own. It had the unintended side effect of taking another step towards independence from Portugal. Being a state was better than a colony but the desire for true freedom was too strong to be ignored or extinguished.

Things were going great in Brazil, but as a result, Portugal was in complete disarray. The country hadn't had a king present in the country for years. King Joao VI and the royal court and family had to return to try and bring order back to their homeland. In 1821 there was a Liberal Revolution.

The Liberal Revolution completely changed the Portuguese, and therefore, the Brazilian political landscape. Revolutionaries replaced the royal governors that King Joao VI left behind in Portugal to rule in his stead. A revolutionary council of regency replaced them and ruled over the country. After their demand that King Joao VI's return was met, they went about displacing him from power. Then they went about completely destroying the monarchy ruling system.

King Joao VI's heir, Prince Pedro didn't go back to Portugal with his father. He stayed in Brazil. Demands were made of Prince Pedro to relinquish control of the country back to its citizens. At first he refused. Eventually he caved in after losing support among his soldiers and politicians.

Famously, on September 7, 1822, Prince Pedro stood upon the banks of the Ipiranga River. There he made an announcement of Brazil's independence after tearing off the Portuguese symbol from his military uniform: "By my blood, by my honor and by God, I will make Brazil free."

With that, three hundred and twenty two years of Brazil being a Portuguese colony ended. It was free. Soon, free from the yoke of another Empire, they would build their own.

THE BRAZILIAN EMPIRE

In the history of Latin America, transitions from colonial rule were often chaotic and violent. Brazil, though far from drama free, didn't suffer those same hardships. For Brazil, independence and the first years after came with little bloodshed.

King Joao VI's son, Prince Pedro, became the first emperor of Brazil. Now known as Dom Pedro I, he was the leader to usher the country into its newborn stage. His rule was met with mixed criticism. Though his decisions were often and rightfully questioned, he also accomplished important milestones in the country's history.

As soon as Emperor Dom Pedro I took his place on the Brazilian throne, he had to stomp out any burning remnants of rebellion from those loyal to Portugal. He spent the first two years dealing with that threat. Perhaps the most famous was his fight and victory against the Confederation of the Equator.

The Confederation of the Equator was a movement of wealthy landowners and secessionists that were opposed to Dome Pedro I's liberal reforms in Brazil. This failed rebellion took place in Pernambuco, Paraiba and

Ceara. And though it failed, it might have inspired later attempts at rebellion against the new Brazilian monarchy.

War was on the horizon in South America. Brazil, which took control of what is now known as Uruguay back in 1817 after wars there between the locals, British and Spanish, was about to find itself embroiled in an armed conflict with its neighbor to the south, Argentina. The Cisplatine War would negatively affect Brazilian-Argentinean relations for centuries to come and usher in a new independent nation.

After gaining its independence in 1822, Brazil faced discontent and unrest in the Banda Oriental area of its small empire. In 1824, Brazil and Argentina met to talk about a possible creation of a new nation, Uruguay, which might help quell tensions. That did not work.

Dom Pedro I decided to claim Uruguay for Brazil and send a large force to occupy the new territory. He made moves to try and make it official and on May 9, 1824 declared it the new Cisplatine Province of his fledgling empire. This was less than popular among those who lived in this new Brazilian province.

It took a little time to organize and arm themselves, but on April 19, 1825, Uruguayan revolutionaries, led by

Juan Antonio Lavalleja and reinforced by soldiers from Argentina, crossed the River de la Plata and invaded the countryside. They managed to take and hold the area, furthering the conflict to come.

That 1825 invasion, spearheaded by Juan Antonio Lavalleja's men who became known as the "Thirty Three Immortals," mostly succeeded in galvanizing those living in the Cisplatine Province and Uruguay to fight back against Brazil. Thousands of supports joined the Immortals and prepared for the war to come.

In December 1825, after local leaders in the Banda Oriental declared independence in August, Brazil declared war on Argentina. Brazil claimed that Argentina broke the agreement of neutrality over the region and instigated the fight against Brazil in Uruguay. Things did not go well for the Argentineans during the first year of fighting.

Poorly equipped and not wanting any part of the fight, the Argentine army was at a severe disadvantage against their Brazilian enemies. Brazil's military was better trained, better equipped and larger. Plus, they were bolstered by a nationalist pride that came from only recently being their own country. Still, Argentina eventually started to win the war over Uruguay.

Though poorly equipped at first, the Argentinean people took it upon themselves to help arm their soldiers and provide supplies, improving their morale on the front lines. They began winning battle after battle, all small, but they started to pile up.

If the Cisplatine War was more popular among the Brazilian populace they probably would have been able to stick in there and win the fight. But Dom Pedro I could no longer justify the conflict. The stalemate was too costly in both lives and resources. With intervention from the French and British, Argentina, Brazil and representatives of what would become Uruguay met and agreed to the 1828 Treaty of Montevideo. Hostilities would end and the Cisplatine province would become part of a new nation, the aforementioned Uruguay.

Things were not going well for the first Brazilian Emperor, Dom Pedro I. Many in his own country thought him too liberal, others didn't think him liberal enough. He insisted on fighting the costly Cisplatine War, in which he lost land and gained nothing, which added to his unpopularity. Then the situation in Brazil's former colonial master, Portugal, got more complicated and demanded his attention.

In 1826, Dom Pedro I had to temporarily take the Portuguese crown along with that of Brazil. But he was at war at home and felt his hold in Rio de Janeiro slipping, so he had his daughter, Dona Maria II, rule in Portugal in his stead. His own daughter, however, was usurped that same year by his younger brother, Prince Dom Miguel.

Drama with his royal family in Portugal, the disaster of the Cisplatine War, and a sexual scandal dragged Dom Pedro I's reputation and popularity down into the mud. The Brazilian parliament spent years during his rule debating whether political appointments should be made by the emperor or the legislature, further weakening his rule. And finally his family troubles in Portugal forced him to make a decision between his father country and Brazil. He chose Portugal.

Unable to deal with problems in both Brazil and Portugal simultaneously, Dom Pedro I, first emperor of Brazil, left Rio de Janeiro and South America for the aforementioned Portugal. He left the throne to his son Dom Pedro II on April 7, 1831. In 1832, he led an army and got involved in war in the Iberian Peninsula before succumbing to illness in 1834. Despite his perceived failures in the latter years of his rule in Brazil, he was remembered as a key figure in spreading liberalism in South America and Europe, plus, of course, his most famous action, declaring independence for a new Brazilian nation.

Dom Pedro II was only five years old when he was declared emperor of Brazil. As often the case with rulers far too young to rule, the country was thrown into relative chaos and disarray. The years of 1831 to 1841 became one of the most unstable periods in Brazilian history.

With such a young ruler, not ready to actually rule, Brazil's provinces, leaders and influential politicians, businessmen and even the church fought over regency in the young nation. As the people waited for their rightful emperor to come of age, there was a real lack of leadership, leading to a decade of instability and crisis. Luckily it would come to end on July 23, 1840 when parliament voted the only fourteen year old emperor into office to actively rule.

Dom Pedro II didn't have to wait long before he faced his first true challenges, other than his arranged marriage. The first came in regards to slavery, which was still an active practice in Brazil. Even though it was legally banned in 1826 after an agreement with the British, the illegal trade still thrived. Unhappy that slaves were still being traded against the agreement, the British took action.

The British passed the Aberdeen Act of 1845, which gave British ships the required authority to board and search any Brazilian ships for slaves. If any slaves or sign of slave trading was found on one of these vessels, they would be seized.

The Eusebio de Queiros law was passed on September 4, 1850. It gave the Brazilian government greater powers to fight the illegal slave trade in the country. Quickly they eliminated the existence of slaves in Brazil while appeasing their important British allies.

As Dom Pedro II had to deal with slavers and their dispute with the British, a revolt broke out in Brazil. The Praieira Revolt or Beach Rebellion was a result of leftover tensions after the formation of the Brazilian Empire. Really it was a problem between radical liberals and conservatives in Pernambuco. It never really took off and amounted to much but it did inspire small rebellions in regions throughout the country that the young emperor would have to deal with throughout his reign.

A third major crisis broke out to the south of Brazil. Once again, Brazil found itself entangled in a war against Argentina over the nation of Uruguay. It started with the Argentinean dictator Juan Manuel de Rosas.

Juan Manuel de Rosas had been stoking the fires of rebellions in Uruguay and Brazil from his seat of power in Buenos Aires. Joining forces with the Uruguayans and disenfranchised Argentineans, Dom Pedro II sent Brazilian forces to engage Rosas in the Platine War.

The union between Uruguay and Brazil led to the defeat and ouster of Juan Manuel de Rosas. Having won the Platine War, Dom Pedro II did something his father couldn't, won a war with Argentina. Many credited his cool, calm decision making as a key part of the victory.

Under Dom Pedro II's leadership, Brazil thrived. Like his father before him, he was determined to modernize and industrialize the nation. He succeeded in increasing its prestige not only in South America but on the world stage. Though far from perfect, he was a popular leader.

Dom Pedro II was Brazil's emperor during South America's bloodiest conflict, the Paraguayan War. The complex conflict was boiled down to Brazil's alliance with Uruguay and Argentina against a power mad dictator in Paraguay, Francisco Solano Lopez. Ending in 1876, the war cost Paraguay more than any of the three other countries involved. Francisco Solano Lopez was among the couple hundred thousand Paraguayans who died over the course of the long war. And the country had a large portion of its lands divided up by the victors.

Like he did in the Platine War, Dom Pedro II's steadfast leadership helped Brazil once again prevail in a major armed conflict. But his victories were not restricted to the battlefield. He won plenty on the political and social theaters.

Under Dom Pedro II, Brazil was seen as the most progressive and modern country behind only the United States. Chief among his goals, other than the modernization of his country, was the end of what he saw as a stain on Brazil's growing good reputation: slavery. Though his agreement with the British when he was younger helped stem the illegal slave trade, he was dedicated to completely abolishing the practice.

Calling for an end to slavery was a risky move by Dom Pedro II. Slavery was so entrenched in Brazilian society from rich to poor that he faced opposition to its end at every turn. In his "Speech from the Throne" in 1867, he urged for a gradual end to slavery, knowing his country's addiction and dependence on slaves couldn't be ended cold turkey, lest he wanted civil war. Many saw it as political suicide but he stuck to his guns and his beliefs. Victory did come in the form of the Law of Free Birth, passed on September 28, 1871 making every child born to slaves from that day forth, free men and women.

Though Dom Pedro II was a mostly beloved leader who would go on to be admired by history, he was still an emperor. All emperors and empires fall. He was no exception.

Discontent grew in Brazil as Dom Pedro II's enthusiasm for his country waned. The very idea of a monarchy began to sour not only on Brazilians but the entire world. Successful revolution and rebellion from dictator and royal rule started in the United States and spread throughout the world during the following century. Whispers of the possible end of the empire started to spread.

By 1887, Dom Pedro II had grown gravely ill. He had to travel to Milan, Italy to get treatment that was unavailable in Brazil. For two weeks he teetered on the edge of death. But while courting the grim reaper on his sick bed, Dom Pedro II heard news of his greatest victory. On May 22, 1888, slavery was completely abolished in Brazil. When he returned to his country in better health he was welcomed as a hero and as a beloved leader. It seemed for a little while that the Brazilian monarchy's population was not unflappable and at the height of its power.

Ignoring the desires of the Brazilian people, politicians and the military turned against Dom Pedro II and his empire. After a coup d'état , Brazil was no longer considered a monarchy but instead declared a republic on November 15, 1889. He did not fight it, he did not resist it. In an unprecedented rational reaction, he simply abdicated the throne and willingly went into exile with his family until his death on December 5, 1891.

Dom Pedro II's legacy on the world stage and in the history of Brazil is and will always likely be a positive one. His efforts abolished slavery, eliminated a lot of the inequality among the citizens, greatly improved the infrastructure and quality of life, won important wars, introduced republican and democratic ideals and made Brazil a true world power. He raised the country from childhood to adulthood. It could easily be argued that he was the best and most effective leader that Brazil has ever had, even to this day.

THE REPUBLIC

After Dom Pedro II was disposed via coup d'état on November 15, 1889, Brazil was governed as a republic, led by the coup leader General Deodoro da Fonseca, who became the first president. It was technically a constitutional democracy but there were still restrictions on voting and participation for women and the illiterate who made up the country's majority.

The first presidencies of the Brazilian Republic were headed by military men, elected into office. But this changed in 1894. Landowners and coffee farmers gained power through the vote and led to a period from the 1890s to the 1930s where different factions and aspects of society vied for the presidency, sometimes peacefully, sometimes violently but never by civil war.

During this time of the Old Brazilian Republic, the country took a fairly loose isolationist policy, for example, their policies during World War I at the beginning of the twentieth century.

At the outbreak of World War I, Brazil remained neutral. Though it was allied with countries on the allied side of the war, it didn't participate. Brazil officially declared its neutrality on August 4, 1914, hoping not to interfere with its participation in international trade, especially when it came to its biggest cash crop, coffee. And it stayed that way for almost two years until the sinking of a Brazilian ship by a German submarine.

On May 3, 1916, a Brazilian merchant ship, Rio Branco, was struck and sunk by a German submarine launched torpedo. Even though citizens were outraged by this, the attack happened in restricted waters, under a British flag and the crew was mostly Norwegian. So nothing was done. Then Germany utilized a policy of unrestricted submarine warfare.

New German policies during World War I led to the April 5, 1917 sinking of the Brazilian ship Parana. Loaded with coffee, it was sunk and three Brazilian citizens were killed in the torpedo attack. That triggered a chain of events that led to Brazil involvement in the war.

Protests broke out all over Brazil but mostly in the capital. The citizenry was outraged at the attack on the Parana and demanded justice. That snowballed into violence and assaults on shops and stores owned by Germanic peoples living in Brazil. Some politicians were forced to resign. And when it came down to it, the government had no choice but to give in to the wishes of the people. In October 1917, Brazil declared war on Germany and its allies.

The involvement of the Brazilian Army in World War I was very limited. Ground troops weren't sent to Europe but a small force of officers was. They fought alongside and aided the French forces on the front lines.

Unlike the army, the Brazilian Navy was more heavily and directly involved in the fighting in World War I. Mostly focused on finding and destroying German submarines, a naval force was sent to patrol the waters along the Western African coastline. Their effectiveness was compromised by the lack of agreement among the allies of how the Brazilian Navy should be used and where it should've been deployed.

Having suffered few casualties in World War I, Brazil made it out of the conflict mostly unscathed. In fact, it was the years right after the war when the country actually benefited from the war. A need for goods in Europe, ravaged by war, started a spike in industrialization in Brazil to fill the gap left by the continent's countless destroyed cities and factories.

The 1930s brought massive industrial and agricultural growth to Brazil. But this increase in prosperity did not mean that everything was peaceful and calm within the country. Most notably, the Republic was overtaken by a military junta led by Getulio Vargas. This military-headed regime ruled the country from 1930-1945, but it did not go unopposed.

Two major oppositions and challenges to Getulio Vargas's military rule over Brazil grew under the strict regime. The first, known as the Constitutionalist Revolution of 1932, was started by the murder of protesting university students in Sao Paulo. The state of Sao Paulo rose up and rebelled against the government. About eighty seven days of fighting, 1,200 deaths (the actual number is unknown) and an almost destroyed state later, Vargas's regime won.

Today, residents of Sao Paulo celebrate the failed revolution every July 9. Though it didn't result in victory, it's seen as the greatest movement in its civic history. And it was the first attempt to fight back against the increasingly unpopular Getulio Vargas regime.

Both communists and fascist movements in Brazil attempted coup d'état against Getulio Vargas's regime. Both failed but the increasingly brazen attempts to overthrow the military government started to signal the end. Though it continued for about a decade, it was a decade marred by growing hatreds and stricter, more vicious reprisals.

Life in Brazil became more complicated during the onset of World War II and the years following it. That all started with the man in power who was approaching the status of an authoritarian dictator, Getulio Vargas. From 1937-1945, the Estado Novo, or "New State," was installed in Brazil cementing his status as dictator.

As German military aggression in Europe, Mussolini's fascist rule in Italy and Japanese expansion in Asia increased, the status of Brazil's alliances became blurry. The Axis powers wanted the Estado Novo and Getulio Vargas to join them, considering shared values and styles of rule. From 1933-1938 Germany was the main consumer of Brazilian cotton and was the second-largest importer of their coffee products. The German Bank opened hundreds of branches in Brazil. Both countries had extensive military and civilian trade networks that made it hard not to side with Germany, even after the rise of the Nazis. All the while, the United States and Allied powers worried about that growing relationship in the Southern hemisphere.

Not willing to just let Brazil join the Axis Powers, the United States reached out to the country and the Estado

Novo in 1940. The United States brought what they knew Brazil needed and what the Axis Powers couldn't supply as much of: money and trade opportunities.

First, the United States agreed to loan Brazil large amounts of money that it could use to further industrialize the interior of the country. In return, Brazil would supply the US with one essential supply it needed for the war: rubber. This lucrative partnership had consequences, though.

After Brazil broke diplomatic relations with Nazi Germany in 1942, at the insistence of the United States, Hitler ordered increased offensive activities in the ocean and air around South America. Hundreds of Brazilians died from Nazi and Italian submarine attacks on Brazilian vessels. So with no other choice, Getulio Vargas and the country declared war against the Axis powers on August 22, 1942. And unlike World War I, Brazil actually sent troops to fight in the Italian theater of war.

The dam of the Estado Novo, holding back political and popular discontent, was near breaking on the outbreak of World War II. During the war, Brazil's policies and decisions were at odds with the reality at home. People couldn't square away Gestulio Vargas's authoritarian dictator regime with him siding with the Allied Forces in the war.

Gestulio Vargas tried to appease the want for more liberal policies and the easing of the government's boots on the citizenry neck. He promised "a new postwar era of liberty." This new era was meant to give amnesty to political prisoners, free elections and remove the laws against his opposition parties, including the communists. His own easing of policies also led to the end of his reign over Brazil. Vargas's own administration forced him out of office on October 29, 1945.

Much like its neighbor to the south, Argentina, Brazil also had a dirty secret after World War II. Influential and high ranking Nazi Officers and personnel were given sanctuary by the significant German population in the country. Gestulio Vargas' government also had sympathy towards them and was thought to provide some protections to these war criminals. Infamous war criminal and one of the worst human beings to have ever lived, Josef Mengele, was one of the monsters who found a safe haven in Brazil.

Democracy returned to Brazil after the forced resignation of Gestulio Vargas. That did not keep the former ruler on the bench for long though. He returned to politics in 1951 and was re-elected via a secret ballot. There were several reasons why he was able to return. The blame was at the feet of the Eurico Dutra presidency.

Eurica Dutra was elected into office after Gestulio Vargas. Even though the Vargas Estado Novo violated human rights and was authoritarian, the Brazilian economy prospered. Dutra, who relied too heavily on US aid and money, then wasted it, plunging the country into an economic crisis.

Brazilians forgot about the many negatives of Gestulio Vargas's regime and yearned for the prosperity of the Estado Novo and the sense of national pride they felt. Though Vargas did succeed in stopping dependency on foreign resources and founded Brazilian Petroleum, his last reign would not last very long.

A series of disastrous schemes exposed on behalf of Gestulio Vargas turned the military, his muscle, against him. His attempts to regain their trust and support failed. Knowing that his time was over, Vargas fatally shot himself in the chest on August 24, 1954. It would be great to say that was the last of dictators and military authoritarian regimes in Brazil, but sadly that is not the case.

MODERN BRAZIL

In the decade from 1954-1964, Brazil continued to hold democratic elections though there was a lot of fighting, conflicts, attempted coup d'états and revolutions. It would seem that the country just couldn't find peace. Witnessing all this, the Brazilian military decided to take it upon themselves to get things under control and take over leadership.

Using the fear of communism and the rise of the left, the Brazilian military staged a successful coup d'état. After the sitting president Joao Goulart was removed from office, Army Chief of Staff Marshal Humberto de Alencar Castelo Blanco became interim president. Castelo Blanco ruled as opposition politicians were removed from their offices. But he had no intention of staying in his top seat. Though he stayed a little longer than he wanted, he did abdicate his position.

The iron fist didn't come until Castelo Blanco's successor, General Artur da Costa e Silva. Brazil's political system, always seemingly influx, changed when he passed the Fifth Institutional Act, on December 13, 1968. Not only did this give the president dictator-like powers, it broke up congress, state legislatures, suspended the country's constitution and gave him and his regime power to impose brutal censorship against any opposition.

General Artur de Costa e Silva's rule had serious ramifications but did not last long. He had to leave office after suffering a stroke in 1969. Under the new rules imposed by him, the vice president didn't inherit the presidency, the military did. General Emilio Garrastazu Medici became the new leader of Brazil.

Much like the brutal authoritarian leaders of Brazil's past, General Medici was both a monster and beloved at the same time. This mercurial reign made bringing an end to his regime's countless human rights abuses difficult. Especially since the world's most powerful country, the United States, backed them in the name of stopping the spread of communism in South America.

General Medici's rule was one of terror, including secret arrests, torture and persecution without trials of journalists, opposition leaders and anyone who spoke out against his military dictatorship. In response, groups of guerrilla rebels would kidnap and even murder members of his regime. That just intensified the terror.

At the same time as General Medici's government ran rough shot over any human decency, the economy benefited. Brazil's national team won the 1970 World Cup. And he enacted the First National Development Plan. This schizophrenic government was a running theme throughout Brazilian history since the onset of the twentieth century. In 1974, General Ernesto Geisel was "elected."

General Geisel continued many of the policies of his predecessor. His focus was on continuing to strengthen the economy and crush the protesters and guerrilla fighters who continued to resist the military regime. Though he was not as brutal as Medici, he didn't lift the boot too much off Brazil's throat.

Nothing terrible lasts forever. Neither did this period of military dictatorship. A civil unrest movement, called the Diretas Ja, started. They put on a series of protests demanding direct, uncorrupted, democratic elections. With the world's attention and the slowly loosening noose of oppression already being eased, they only partially succeeded. They did not get the direct vote but the presidency was returned to civilians, no more military.

The horrors of the military regime largely went unpunished. But they did not go forgotten. The Comissao de Direitos Humanos e Assistencia Juridica da Ordem dos Advogados do Brasil puts the number of people disappeared and/or murdered by the Brazilian military regimes during this period at three hundred and thirty three. Those are just the ones they know about. Many times that number were tortured and kidnapped, held without trial or due process.

Unfortunately corruption and the gross abuse of power still have not left the highest government offices in Brazil. Even today the public is hesitant to trust them, and rightfully so. There are still divides among those who do and don't support whichever regime is in charge.

Brazil is a country that has seen tremendous growth over the years. Today, in the early twenty-first century, Brazil is a legitimate world power. It has one of the world's largest and fastest growing economies. Businesses, innovators and the sciences have flocked to the country. So has hope.

The world saw tensions in Brazil before and during the controversial 2014 Fifa World Cup and the 2016 Summer Olympics, both held in country. Tensions in the host cities, in the favelas, lower income areas, and the government rose and almost reached a fever pitch. Police and military were sent into the most "dangerous" neighborhoods to pacify them and neutralize any gang or criminal activity making it safer for the throngs of World

Cup and Olympics attendees. Protests at home and abroad may not have stopped anything but shined a light on some of the same problems Brazil has today.

Home to the largest section of the Amazon Rainforest and River, one of the most diverse countries in the world and an epicenter of culture, Brazil is one of the planet's jewels. Threatened by climate change and corruptible governments, its rise to the forefront on the world's stage isn't guaranteed. But if nothing else, as shown by its history, Brazil does move forward, especially when faced with hardship.

SOURCES

https://brewminate.com/a-history-of-brazil-from-the-precolonial-era-to-the-kingdom-period/

https://www.zum.de/whkmla/sp/0910/hersheys/hersheys3.html

https://historycollection.co/day-history-pinzon-discovers-brazil-1530/

https://en.wikipedia.org/wiki/Duarte_Pacheco_Pereira

https://exploration.marinersmuseum.org/subject/pedro-alvares-cabral/

https://www.globalsecurity.org/military/world/war/platine.htm

https://brazilian.report/guide-to-brazil/2017/09/25/colonial-brazil/

https://www.britannica.com/topic/Estado-Novo-Brazilian-history

http://www.localhistories.org/brazil.html

http://www.geographia.com/brazil/brazihistory.htm

https://en.wikipedia.org/wiki/History_of_Brazil

https://www.miningweekly.com/article/the-brazilian-gold-rush-2012-10-12

https://library.brown.edu/create/fivecenturiesofchange/chapters/chapter-1/gold-discovered/

https://www.historytoday.com/archive/brazil-first-world-war

https://brazilian.report/guide-to-brazil/2017/10/15/brazil-world-war-ii/

https://www.theclassroom.com/brazilian-involvement-wwii-12185.html

https://library.brown.edu/create/brazilundervargas/

Printed in Great Britain
by Amazon